Original title:
Maple Musings

Copyright © 2025 Creative Arts Management OÜ
All rights reserved.

Author: Zachary Prescott
ISBN HARDBACK: 978-1-80567-211-1
ISBN PAPERBACK: 978-1-80567-510-5

Reflections on a Fallen Leaf

A leaf fell down with quite a flair,
It twirled and spun, fell through the air.
I watched it land with such great style,
And thought, perhaps, it needs a trial.

It landed soft on a dog below,
The pup just barked, then put on a show.
With wagging tail, it started to dance,
While I just sat, amazed at the chance.

A squirrel then saw the show unfold,
He grabbed the leaf, all daring and bold.
But in a flash, he slipped and skidded,
Leaving me in laughter, I was a kid.

The wind then laughed, it tossed them about,
A swirling mess, no care or doubt.
Nature's humor, a comic relief,
A wisdom shared through this fallen leaf.

The Last Warmth of Day

As the sun bows down with flair,
Leaves laugh, dancing through the air.
Squirrels plotting their nutty spree,
While I hunt for my lost keys.

Breezes tickle my chilly nose,
Whispers of spiced pumpkin prose.
The sky turns blush, a fleeting show,
And my hat flies off; where'd it go?

Soliloquy of the Understory

In the thicket, critters debate,
Whose turn is it to navigate?
A raccoon claims it's time to feast,
While a fox dreams of a lovely beast.

Moss giggles under a toadstool hat,
With a snail that thinks he's far too fat.
"Why race?" says the owl from his perch,
"Just enjoy this cozy search!"

Chasing Shadows of Change

Jackets collude on the grass below,
Like lost puppies in a chilly show.
"Guess you're mine for a breezy ride!"
Pants flapping like they're filled with pride.

Wind whispers secrets, trees sway along,
A butterfly's dance, a playful song.
Fleeting moments before they freeze,
Nature's laughter carried on the breeze.

Sipping on Autumn's Brew

Cider bubbles in my cup so bright,
Dancing leaves throw a wild delight.
Cupcakes swirl with frosting galore,
Baking battles ignite, who wants more?

Around the bonfire, jokes ignite,
Marshmallow monsters take their flight.
With every sip, we share and cheer,
Laughter echoes, autumn's here!

Foliage Fantasies

In a forest of dreams, leaves spin,
Squirrels dance, let the fun begin.
Acorns fall, with a bang and a plop,
Watch out below, don't let your snack drop!

Chasing branches, I lost my shoe,
The trees giggle, as if they knew.
Whispers of leaves, secrets they tell,
Nature's laughter, a magical spell.

The Roar of Silence

A stillness falls over the glade,
Yet in my head, a parade.
Crickets serenade a bumbling bee,
While mushrooms plot world domination, maybe?

In the quiet, a squirrel sneezes,
Sending leaves tumbling like little breezes.
I chuckle softly, oh what a sight,
Even the trees can't contain their delight.

Winds of Transformation

The wind whispers sweet nothings to me,
Tickling the leaves, wild and free.
A gusty giggle spins around,
As branches sway, joyfully unbound.

Winds of change, they play hide and seek,
Fluttering petals, a comical peek.
Old trees chuckle, what a fuss,
Their roots wiggling like it's a must!

Colors of Solitude

In solitude's hue, I ponder the trees,
Blushing in autumn, swaying with ease.
Golden yellows, fiery reds,
Leaves clapping softly, lifting my spirits like sleds.

A lonely crow sings a tune, quite absurd,
Echoing laughter, oh what a bird!
With every color, a giggle sets free,
Even solitude can dance joyfully.

A Symphony in Red

Leaves dance in spirals, twirling in glee,
Squirrels plot mischief, sipping sweet tea.
Red coats their branches, a bright, bold affair,
Wondering if nature laughs at our hair.

Crackling old leaves, shoes crunching with cheer,
Geese take to the sky, honking quite clear.
They say autumn's here with its playful parade,
While I trip on a twig, how embarrassing! Wait!

Whispered Tales of Autumn

Pumpkins grin wide with teeth made of stone,
I've carved a few faces, but still feel alone.
The corn maze confuses, I'm lost in my thoughts,
Is that the way out or just where I bought?

Flannel shirts outnumber my sweaters times ten,
"Where's the hot cider?" I ask once again.
The trees tell me stories, the wind has a joke,
But I'm still lost here, in fog, coffee, and smoke.

Where Serenity Falls

Leaves flutter like dancers, a soft, silly show,
Giggling branches sway, putting on a glow.
Zen-like I ponder, sipping my brew,
While a squirrel flips me off, how rude but true!

The park bench is comfy, or so they proclaimed,
Until I discover, I'm totally framed.
A family of ducks think I'm food on the run,
I am not a baguette! Wait, is that my bun?

Harmonies of the Harvest

Ripe apples fall down with a thud and a bounce,
I pick them with gusto, as if I could flounce.
But one rolls away, oh joy, what a chase,
It's clear I'm no athlete, just part of this place.

Crisp air is filled with laughter, or is that my wheeze?
Everyone's picking, while I trip on some leaves.
The cider's delightful, it warms my frosty toes,
And the laughs continue, as clumsiness grows.

Hues of the Wind

Leaves dance around, oh what a sight,
Twirling and spinning, a comical flight.
They whisper secrets, in rustling tones,
Telling the stories of acorns and cones.

Squirrels look puzzled, with a nut in hand,
As leaves do their jig, they don't understand.
Pine cones are giggling, high up in their boughs,
While the wind plays a tune, with laughter it vows.

Shimmering Layers

A blanket of colors, layered so thick,
Who needs a painter? Nature's the trick!
Red, gold, and brown, all mixed in a bowl,
Leaves try to cover up, but they all lose control.

With every gust, they flutter and flip,
Stuck in my hair, oh what a big trip!
Each layer a laughter, a prank in disguise,
Fall's comical chaos, a feast for our eyes.

The Essence of Autumn

Pumpkin spice lattes in every hand,
While squirrels chat gossip from their leafy stand.
Frogs wear the best of their fashion this time,
Croaking in rhythm, they think it's sublime.

With jackets too snug, we waddle about,
While our limbs get all tangled, let out a shout!
The essence of autumn, a quirky parade,
With laughter and joy, all worries will fade.

Reflections in Crimson

Puddles reflect a crimson disguise,
A mirror for all, with sparkling eyes.
But watch your step—slips are still planned,
As leaves sing their songs, all over the land.

The trees stand tall, laughing overhead,
While squirrels make plans to mess with your tread.
Reflections of fun, in nature's big show,
In the symphony of fall, we all steal the glow.

Fallen Fables

Leaves are falling, what a sight,
Whispers of stories, taking flight.
I tripped and stumbled, oh what glee,
One leaf laughed, 'Catch me if you see!'

They tumble down in a swirling race,
Each one hides a cheeky face.
With every gust, they twist and twirl,
Nature's prank, a leafy whirl!

Gentle Dances in the Breeze

In the park, the leaves do sway,
Twisting, turning, in disarray.
One leaf called, 'Let's have a ball!'
As they twirled, they began to fall.

A gust of wind, and there they go,
Spinning around, putting on a show.
Laughter echoes through the trees,
As leaves perform with such great ease!

Celestial Rustlings

Stars above with leaves below,
Each soft rustle starts the show.
A leaf yells, 'I'm like a star!'
I replied, 'You won't go far!'

The night is sweet with chuckles bright,
As leaves converse in moonlit light.
'Let's reach for dreams', one leaf said,
But they fall down instead, like lead!

The Secret Life of Leaves

What do they ponder as they flop?
'Should we jump? Or just drop?'
A leaf grinned, 'I'll play the fool!'
'Let's race down to the garden pool!'

They huddle close, in a busy crowd,
Gossiping softly, feeling proud.
'Did you see that fall?' one exclaimed,
And then they all burst out, unclaimed!

Secrets in the Canopy

Leaves whisper tales up high,
Squirrels plot while birds just fly.
Raccoons join in with a laugh,
Nature's comedy on the path.

Branches dance without a care,
While acorns fall and start to glare.
Who knew trees had such wild dreams?
Beneath their shade, the sunlight beams.

A wind-up joke, a rustling sound,
The forest floor, a merry ground.
Hiding nuts is quite the tease,
Who knew it'd lead to such a breeze?

Crackle and pop, a million hues,
Nature's giggles, free to choose.
In this green theater up so high,
Leaves wave hello, and squirrels sigh.

A Tapestry of Fall

Orange and red, the colors clash,
As leaves dramatize their final flash.
Who knew trees could throw a show?
A leaf ballet in sun's warm glow.

Cider boats on autumn streams,
Sipping from nature's silly dreams.
The pumpkins giggle, round and bright,
Planning mischief each crisp night.

The scarecrows stand with goofy grins,
Counting down to Halloween wins.
Mummies shiver, winds agree,
As owls hoot, 'Hey, look at me!'

Fallen laughter paints the ground,
In this symphony, joy is found.
Nature's quilt, stitched with delight,
Wraps us warmly throughout the night.

The Sweetness of Decay

Crunching leaves beneath my feet,
Wasted leftovers, oh what a treat!
Apples drop with little *thuds*,
Nature's candy, a bit of spuds.

Fruits gone rogue, with smiles wide,
Dancing in the breeze with pride.
Forget the pies, the peels rebel,
As squirrels claim their fruity shell.

Cinnamon spills from a crook's arm,
As nature plays its charming charm.
A pie left out is never shy,
Chocolate whispers 'Give me a try!'

The ground adorned with crispy trails,
With awkward jokes in nature's tales.
Decay's sweet kiss, a final flair,
A giggle hidden everywhere.

Harvesting Memories

Baskets full of laughter, cheer,
Each tuck and roll, we bring it near.
Cornfields chuckle as we run,
Shucking jokes, oh, what fun!

Grandma's recipes, secrets awake,
Mixing smiles in every cake.
Our hands all sticky, flour flies,
Who knew baking could bring such highs?

Ghosts of summers fade away,
But memories linger, come what may.
Autumn hugs us in its fold,
With stories shared and love retold.

Each moment snatched, a golden prize,
We harvest joy through playful skies.
In every bite, our hearts engage,
As laughter writes the perfect page.

In the Heart of the Grove

In the grove where we giggle,
Leaves dance like a party with no wiggle.
Squirrels gossip with cheeks so round,
Sharing secrets, all around.

A acorn fell, a squirrel slipped,
Into a puddle, his pride he gripped.
Laughter echoes as we all stare,
Who knew trees had such flair?

The wind sings songs that tickle our ears,
As branches sway, bringing forth cheers.
We jump and twirl, what a sight,
Even the owls stay up at night!

Underneath the funny old sprout,
We make wishes, no doubt about.
In the heart of the grove, so bright,
Life is silly, pure delight!

Crimson Whispers

Crimson leaves whisper, hey, look here!
A leaf falls, it's a non-fear spear!
With a flutter and a twist,
Fall comes, and it can't be missed.

Beneath the apple, a pie was found,
An old crow tried to dance just around.
He bobbed and weaved, what a sight!
Guess he thought he was quite alright!

Pumpkin patches hide their seeds,
Finding them is among our needs.
A scarecrow's hat just took a trip,
It better watch for pumpkin's grip!

Laughter lingers, joy in the air,
Nature's humor, a playful affair.
In every whisper, a chuckle we find,
Crimson secrets, so well-defined!

Autumn's Embrace

In autumn's arms, we find our bliss,
With crunchy leaves that beg for a kiss.
I tripped on a vine, fell down with cheer,
A small worm laughed, wriggled near.

The pumpkins grin, their eyes so bright,
While candy corn dances in pure delight.
Goblins in costumes roam the night,
Chasing shadows in the moonlight.

A cat in a hat, oh what a scene,
Claims to be a Halloween queen!
While bats are squawking a silly song,
We join in, it won't be long!

Cider flows with jokes from the best,
As we sip and laugh, feeling blessed.
Autumn wraps us in giggles and grace,
A season of joy, a happy embrace!

Leafy Reveries

In leafy dreams where stories bloom,
A chicken crossed, does it lead to doom?
With a twirl and a flap, it danced that day,
In the chorus of leaves, hip-hip-hooray!

Little bugs throw a disco ball,
On a branch, they invite us all.
Caterpillars twirl in feathered shoes,
While crickets play, sharing tunes.

A leaf fell down, bright orange in flight,
It landed on my head, what a sight!
I strutted around like a funny king,
With autumn's crown, I felt like a fling.

Join us now in this leafy jest,
Beneath the trees, we're truly blessed.
Laughter and joy in nature's prime,
In leafy reveries, we lose track of time!

Nature's Golden Hour

Golden leaves dance in the breeze,
Squirrels plotting, as if they tease.
A pumpkin spice latte spills on the ground,
Nature giggles; oh, what a sound.

Sunshine winks, as shadows play,
Wandering dogs join the fray.
Birds argue over a twig's last piece,
Who knew nature could be a comedic lease?

Frolicking fawns join the show,
Wobbling like they just hit a low.
The trees sway gently, laughing too,
As the wind whispers secrets anew.

But watch your step on this carpet laid,
Or you'll find yourself, in a leaf parade!
With each crunch beneath our feet,
Autumn's humor feels so sweet.

Earthly Elegance

Dressed in hues of orange and gold,
Trees stand tall, their stories told.
But wait, who dropped that acorn there?
Nature's runway has a quirky flair.

A turkey struts in feathery pride,
While chipmunks squabble, refusing to hide.
The elegance, oh, what a sight!
But who knew squirrels could start a fight?

Wind blows softly, wearing a hat,
Taking off with a cat—a true acrobat!
Leaves do the tango, swirling around,
Nature's elegance is comedy bound.

So twirl your scarf and join the fun,
Under the glow of the setting sun.
Bring your laughter, bring your cheer,
Earth has its own stand-up here!

The Art of Letting Go

Leaves drop lightly, with a chuckle,
Nature's way of saying 'no struggle.'
The trees shake off their summer attire,
Whispering secrets as they conspire.

A breeze comes by, smooth as a brush,
Dancing leaves in a whimsical hush.
"Let it go," they seem to giggle,
As around we twist and jiggle.

Critters watch with a knowing wink,
"Why hold on tight? Just let it shrink."
Who knew dropping weight could bring such fun?
In nature's game, we all can run.

Letting go is the best freefall,
Laughing leaves catch us, one and all.
So shed your burdens, laugh out loud,
With nature's jesters, let's feel proud!

Stories in the Twilight

As the sun dips, the stars collide,
Whispers of evening start to glide.
Crickets chirp, they've something to say,
While fireflies dance in a glowing ballet.

A sleepy owl gives a knowing nod,
As children's whispers draw in the odd.
"What's that sound?" and "Where's the light?"
The tales unfold, bringing pure delight.

Bats zoom past, plotting their route,
While the moon pops out with a playful shout.
Nature's stories in dusk's embrace,
A comedy show in this charming place.

So gather close, lend an ear,
For evening fables, far and near.
In the twilight, laughter ignites,
With stories woven in delightful sights.

Wandering Through the Woods

In the woods where squirrels play,
Trees dance like they're in a ballet.
I tripped on roots, oh what a sight,
Even the owls had a laugh that night.

A raccoon stole my sandwich snack,
While I was busy, he made his attack.
Chasing him around a tiny tree,
Who knew forest life was the place to be?

Leaves gossip like they're old friends,
Telling tales of the latest trends.
A butterfly stole my favorite hat,
Now I'm left looking quite the twat.

So off I wander, with no regret,
In this woodland, my laughter is set.
Nature's quirks in every glance,
Who knew an adventure could be so prance!

The Nature of Change

Trees blush red, then drop their clothes,
Seasons flip like a silly pose.
Hot cocoa spills on my warm, soft shirt,
Winter's wind gives a playful spurt.

Spring blooms up with giggles and cheer,
But pollen's here; oh dear, oh dear!
Sneezing, wheezing, I dance in place,
A wild chase for tissues — what a race!

Summer brings ice cream, sticky bliss,
Melting faster than a promised kiss.
The sun laughs as I dodge the sting,
Jump in the pool—let's do this thing!

Autumn glows, but watch your step,
Crunchy leaves, a joyful rep.
Each season has its goofy flair,
Nature's comedy show is always there!

Citrus and Spice Dreams

In dreams where oranges wear little hats,
Lemon trees swing with tiny chats.
Ginger root dances on my bed,
Twirling round like it's the latest trend.

Cinnamon rolls tumble and spin,
"Join the party!" they shout with a grin.
Nutmeg sneezes—oh, bless you, spice!
In this world, everything's nice!

I pour a smoothie that starts to sing,
Bananas jump—what a curious thing!
Mangoes giggle like they've cracked a joke,
Playing pranks, oh what a hoax!

So we'll feast on fun with zest galore,
These fruity friends, who could ask for more?
In citrus dreams where flavors collide,
Join this joyride, let's slip and slide!

The Spirit of the Seasons

The sun and snow play peek-a-boo,
While I wear boots and a sandal too.
Seasons giggle, in a playful dance,
Their silly games put me in a trance.

Winter whispers with frosty breath,
"Do you dare to challenge death?"
But I'd rather build a snowman tight,
With a carrot nose that gives me fright!

Spring skips in, with rain to greet,
Jumping puddles on tiny feet.
Flowers raise their heads so high,
Chasing butterflies as they flutter by.

Summer laughs from the beachy shore,
While I'm sunburnt, yelling for more.
Autumn winks, while the kids all yell,
"Watch out for pumpkins, they cast a spell!"

Each season's pranks will make you smile,
Join the fun, stay for a while.
Life's a circus, wild and bright,
In nature's jest, everything feels right!

Tapestry of Amber

In the park, leaves do dance,
Dressed in colors, take a chance.
Squirrels plotting, sneaky schemes,
Mixing nuts with autumn dreams.

Chasing shadows, laughter loud,
Walking through this leafy crowd.
One leaf flutters, hits my nose,
Time to run, who knows where it goes?

A picnic spread with treats galore,
Baguettes and cheese, oh what a score!
But ants arrive, a tiny swarm,
Stealing snacks, they think it's charm.

As sunset paints the sky so grand,
Beneath this tree, I take a stand.
With every rustle, whispers cheer,
This autumn fun, oh how I steer!

The Rustling Treetops

Whispers ride the evening breeze,
Treetops gossip, with such ease.
Who ate the berries, who stole the pie?
A raccoon culprit? Oh my, oh my!

Branches bending, secrets shared,
Leaves are laughing, none are scared.
I toss a stick and hear a shout,
A squirrel's grumbling roundabout.

Bamboo sticks and toadstool chairs,
Camping here, no worldly cares.
Spiders spinning webs so fine,
Joining me for tea and brine.

When shadows grow and stars emerge,
I can feel the laughter surge.
Nature's circus, join the fun,
With leafy friends till day is done!

Saffron Dreams

Crispy edges, leaves in piles,
Making forts with cheeky smiles.
A leap of faith, I take a dive,
Into the crunch, oh, how I thrive!

Tickling toes in golden hues,
Searching for those hidden clues.
Goblins hiding in plain sight,
In the amber glow of night.

Funny hats of autumn's thrift,
Worn by squirrels, a perfect gift.
Knobbly noses, silly grins,
Frolicking in fall, let the fun begin!

As twilight fades and shadows grow,
I hear the rustling leaves' soft flow.
In this playground, we all gleam,
Dancing through our saffron dream!

Whispering Canopies

Underneath the leafy dome,
Where giggles sprout and feelings roam.
A chipmunk's song, a harmony,
We dance around like we're so free.

Ghostly sounds of rustling fun,
Leaves conspire, one by one.
"Catch me if you can!" they tease,
Racing shadows in the breeze.

With acorns launching through the air,
Who knew nature's pranks could dare?
Falling down, a soft thud sound,
A fluffy tail spins round and round.

When moonlight bathes the merry eve,
And branches sway, I do believe,
These canopies of laughter bright,
Will continue well into the night!

Nature's Paintbrush

Leaves splash bright in the air,
Orange and yellow everywhere.
Squirrels scamper, try to race,
While avoiding the spider's face.

The wind laughs through rustling trees,
Tickling branches with playful tease.
Acorns fall with a gentle thud,
Who knew they could cause such a flood?

Jackets worn though it feels like fall,
But a cat in the sun thinks otherwise at all.
A leaf lands right on my nose!
I must learn to duck - goodness knows!

Nature's canvas, an artful spree,
Always keeps us laughing, you see!
With each twist and turn in the breeze,
We find humor in life's little tease.

The Dance of Orange

In the orchard, fruit takes flight,
Dancing around with all their might.
Pumpkin twirls, a funny sight,
While apples form a conga line so bright.

Carrots join in, doing the cha-cha,
Radishes giggle, 'Oh la la!'
Even the parsnips try to groove,
Just watch those roots, make their move!

Fall's a party, lively and loud,
Nature's animals gather a crowd.
Who knew that veggies were such fun?
This harvest dance has just begun!

With every step, the laughter grows,
In fields adorned with autumn's prose.
Nature's theater under the sun,
A silly waltz, everyone's spun!

Caramelized Dreams

Drizzled leaves like candy sweet,
Sugar-coated paths, a treat!
Bouncing around in sugar high,
Even the clouds go puffing by.

Crispy treats, a golden hue,
Sugar rush for squirrelly crew.
They hop, they skip, they twirl with glee,
Diving into pies, that's the key!

The wind whispers like a warm tease,
While squirrels start to chant with ease.
"More pie!" they squeak, "We want it all!"
As leaves like confetti start to fall.

In laughter's glimmer, joy sets the scene,
As every critter lives the dream.
Caramel drizzles on autumn's cheer,
Nature's dessert, let's all grab a beer!

Amber Hues at Dusk

As twilight wraps the sky in gold,
Creatures sip tea, stories unfold.
Chirping crickets toss in a jest,
Adventures from dusk become the best.

The sun dips low, the owls take flight,
Offering shadows in the twilight.
Fireflies dance, a sparkling show,
Buzzing about in a shimmering flow.

A raccoon stumbles, trips on a twig,
While the frogs ribbit, doing a jig.
Laughter echoes through the trees,
As night brings tales like a gentle breeze.

Amber hues spill dreams in the air,
Silhouettes prancing without a care.
Nature's comedy, we all must embrace,
In the twilight's waltz through a twinkling space.

Autumn Whispers

Squirrels dance, on branches high,
Chasing acorns, oh my, oh my!
The leaves gossip, in hues so bright,
"Who wore it best? That tree or that sight?"

The pumpkins chuckle, round and plump,
Wobbling on steps with a giant thump.
While ghosts giggle in the chilly air,
Is it Halloween or a festive fair?

Cider flows, with laughter near,
As we toast to autumn, loud and clear.
Nature's circus, in shades of gold,
Who knew that falling could be so bold?

So let's embrace the breezy fun,
With every leaf dropped, a new one spun.
For in this season, joy takes flight,
Autumn whispers, "What a silly sight!"

Crimson Reflections

In the mirror of a puddle, I see,
A leaf that's laughing – could that be me?
Dressed in red, it twirls on cue,
"Catch me if you can, I've things to do!"

The wind imitates a sneaky thief,
Stealing hats with such comic relief.
As the squirrels ponder their nutty scheme,
Imagining trees with fluffy ice cream!

A shout from above, "Don't miss the show!"
As twigs and berries begin to throw,
A party of colors, it's quite the bash,
Each leaf a performer, a brilliant splash.

With every rustle, the ground does quake,
The dance of autumn, oh for goodness' sake!
We laugh at nature's hilarious spree,
In this season, there's never a dull tree!

Leaves Unraveled

Leaves gather round for a chat so frank,
"Did you see that branch? What a silly prank!"
Shouting of colors, they spill and slide,
A carnival of shades with nowhere to hide.

Their tales of wind are quite absurd,
"I once flew high just like a bird!"
A leaf who thought it could soar like a kite,
But landed too close to a muddy bite.

The critters giggle at this leaf's tale,
"As if we're not all on nature's scale!"
Amongst the chaos, there's laughter sweet,
As autumn's charms paint our life's beat.

So let's not fret as we tumble down,
For every leaf gets a sparkly crown.
In this wild patchwork, we'll find our way,
Leaves unraveled, we're here to play!

In the Shade of Ruby

Beneath the trees, where shadows prance,
A hide-and-seek game starts by chance.
The sun peeks through with a playful tease,
Making us giggle while teasing the breeze.

A squirrel in shades waits for his cue,
Decked in acorns, the latest debut.
While birds squawk tunes that sound quite weird,
Are they singing, or just plain cheered?

Rakes are ready for the grand fall show,
To pile up leaves in a wiggly row.
But nature laughs with a twist and a whirl,
As a gust of wind causes quite the swirl!

In these vibrant hues, we skip and hop,
Autumn's a jester, with no sign to stop.
So join the laughter, don't be a newbie,
For fun unfolds in the shade of ruby!

Where Shadows Play

In the park where we gather, leaves swirl and sway,
A squirrel took my sandwich, oh what a display!
He danced on the branch, so light on his feet,
As I watched in dismay, he strutted to eat.

The shadows twist oddly, in shapes quite absurd,
Like dancing old ladies, or a guitar-playing bird.
A friend with a hat, so tall and so wide,
It keeps falling off, despite all of his pride.

Laughter erupts as we chase shadows 'round,
Our antics unplanned, in pure joy we bound.
But watch out for puddles, we slip and we slide,
Our fun-spirited frolic, can't be kept inside!

As sunlight retreats, we share tales and jest,
With giggles and grins, it's our very best fest.
The squirrels lift their glasses, a toast to the day,
In the park where we gather, where shadows play.

Beyond the Horizon of Gold

Where sunsets ignite and color the sky,
We wander in search of that raspberry pie.
With laughter as our compass, we roll down the hill,
Chasing dreams made of cookies, what a tasty thrill!

The horizon's a canvas, we scribble a plan,
To catch all the giggles, in our foolproof van.
We paint with our voices, in shades oh so bright,
As we belt out our favorites under the moonlight.

In a world made of pranks, we laugh till we ache,
With jelly-filled donuts, our sweet road we make.
The horizon's a promise, a tale far from told,
Of pies and of laughter, beyond dreams of gold.

So come join the revels, let's giggle and run,
In a land made for fools, where the laughter's just begun.
Beyond all the horizons, where the wild things play,
We'll dance in the twilight, till night takes the day.

Radiance of Rebirth

With each spring's awakening, blooms open wide,
The daisies gossip, while bees bumble beside.
Oh, to be a butterfly, light as a breeze,
I'd sip on those flowers, having tea with the trees.

But here comes the rain, with a splash and a splatter,
I slip in my galoshes, down the road, what a clatter!
The puddles reflect me, in poses so grand,
I'm the queen of this chaos, a crown made of sand.

The colors brighten, a riot in bloom,
Each plant shares its secret, a sweet little tune.
The worms tell their stories, how life's quite absurd,
In the garden of laughter, no whispers deterred.

From winter's deep slumber, we rise with a grin,
With poppy-seed dreams, let the frolic begin.
The radiance of jest in each petal we see,
In this carnival of blooms, come dance wild and free.

Poems in Rust

Among the old fences, with stories to share,
I found a red bike, neglected with care.
Rust curls on the handlebars, but oh what a ride,
With squeaks that resound like a laugh from inside.

The leaves whisper secrets, they gossip and grin,
As I pedal through puddles, letting joy creep in.
Each wobbly turn feels like a wild number,
Like a clown on a tightrope, where laughter won't slumber.

The trees clap their branches, a rustling cheer,
As I weave through the trails, with no hint of fear.
Who knew rust could sparkle, in the light of a jest?
In the park, we create our own silly fest.

So come ride this old bike, let's chase down delight,
With poems in rust, we'll spin laughable flight.
Each bump is a punchline, each laugh a reprise,
In the joy of our journey, we discover the prize.

The Sweetness of Surrender

A squirrel stole my sandwich today,
I swore at him, he danced away.
The trees all chuckled, leaves aflutter,
While I grumbled, covered in butter.

The birds were harping their funny tunes,
As acorns dropped like little goons.
I tried to catch 'em, what a sight!
But they just laughed, took off in flight.

Each gust of wind sang silly scents,
Even the worms looked like they'd condense.
I tossed my crumbs, hoping for grace,
But ants formed a line, a parade's pace.

I waved goodbye to my picnic fun,
In this wooded chaos, no one won.
The laughter echoed as I strolled home,
With leaves in my hair, I felt like a gnome.

Whispers Among the Leaves

The wind told secrets, hushed and sweet,
As I tripped over roots, oh, such a feat!
A chipmunk waved, with a nut in tow,
"Do watch your step, or you might just go!"

The trees chimed in with a rustling cheer,
"Welcome, dear human, we've missed you here!"
With branches that jiggled, they couldn't resist,
Making me question if I should exist.

Clouds rolled in like an unruly mob,
I ducked for cover, avoiding a sob.
They rumbled and grumbled, all in a fuss,
While I laughed and acted outrageous with gusto.

In this leafy choir, with laughter so great,
Nature's humor was my perfect fate.
I took a bow to the flora and fauna,
In a world of giggles, my heart danced on ya.

Tinctures of Time

Autumn's tinctures, a palette so bright,
Leaves swirling down, what a charming sight.
I snuck a big sip from a puddle nearby,
"Is this magic juice?" I couldn't deny.

The colors of orange, they tickled my nose,
Even the sun wore a jacket, it knows!
I strolled through the patterns, all curly and round,
In every step, a new joke I found.

The squirrels were hosting a wild pumpkin feast,
While raccoons debated who'd be the least.
I peeked at their gathering, what a grand show!
In woodland town, I felt quite the glow.

With each twist in time, I chuckled away,
Nature's concoctions kept dullness at bay.
As laughter rippled from branch to root,
I tiptoed along, wearing leaves as my suit.

Nature's Farewell Song

The trees sang softly, a quilt of hues,
As I danced awkwardly, dodging leaves like shoes.
A butterfly winked, said "Join the parade!"
But I tripped on a twig, and the plans were delayed.

"Just follow the clouds," the wind did proclaim,
While I pondered the meaning, feeling quite lame.
The cicadas laughed, made my worries dissolve,
In nature's goodbye, my problems involved.

With each rustle and shuffle, I felt like a fool,
But laughter was crafted, my heart was the tool.
A jolly old crow cawed out his best line,
"Life's too short, keep laughing, divine!"

As sunset arrived, painting skies in gold,
I hugged the trees tightly, with stories untold.
Nature's farewell, a playful refrain,
In this wacky embrace, I danced through the lane.

Laid Bare by Time

In the autumn breeze, leaves fall with grace,
Their vibrant hue fades, a worn-out face.
Squirrels gather snacks, with nuts in tow,
While old trees gossip of the days long ago.

The air fills with laughter, a ticklish tease,
As branches shake off their old, dry sneeze.
Pumpkin spice lattes boast their fall reign,
Yet spill on our shirts; oh, what a stain!

Cider drunk, we dance, embracing the chill,
A rustle of leaves, a world kept still.
Under piles of color, we stumble and trip,
Collecting good memories, one clumsy slip.

So here's to the laughter, the joy, and the cheer,
In the swamp of nostalgia, let's freely veer.
With laughter so hearty, and smiles that shine,
We're laid bare by time, yet we're feeling fine!

Roots of Reflection

Beneath the old oak, we sit and think,
As squirrels debate what to eat and drink.
They chatter away, with seeds in their paws,
While we search for wisdom, and pause for applause.

Reflecting on summers, we giggle and grin,
At memories of wild games; oh, where to begin?
With bugs as our foes, we fought valiantly,
Who knew that a firefly could be so fancy?

The roots twist and tangle, just like our tales,
Of backyard adventures and home-cooked scales.
The laughter rings out 'neath the leafy spread,
While dreaming of snacks to be joyfully fed.

So let's raise a toast to the friends of the past,
For laughter unites us, as seasons are cast.
Through roots of reflection, we giggle and sway,
In a world that's unmatched, come join us and play!

The Dance of Decay

Leaves are swirling, they know how to sway,
In a chaotic jig, they frolic and play.
Nature's odd ballet, with branches so bare,
Leaves twirl with a wink; it's a funky affair.

With every cool gust, they dance to the ground,
A rustling chorus, a rhythmic sound.
We laugh at the chaos, all swirling around,
Dancing with leaves, we're joyfully found.

Old pumpkins with smiles, they rot with delight,
Their squishy, soft guts, a gory sight.
Yet laughter erupts, at the sight of the scene,
As we waddle like ducks through the mess in between.

So here's to the fun in our strangely decayed,
With laughter and whimsy, good vibes on parade.
Amidst all the chaos, can't help but stay,
For life's simply splendid in the dance of decay!

Fragrant Fall Memories

Crisp leaves beneath and a warm spiced drink,
The fragrance of autumn makes us all think.
We gather our friends, with laughter galore,
As pumpkin patches beckon, who could ask for more?

Candles flicker gently, in homes filled with cheer,
As stories resurrect what we hold most dear.
The crunch of the leaves, oh what a delight,
While we nudge the cat, for a cozy goodnight.

With bonfire stories of ghosts and of fright,
We roast little marshmallows till they melt in our sight.
The taste of hot cider, our warm fall embrace,
While giggles erupt in the glowing dark space.

So gather your friends, lift a glass, take a sip,
For fragrant fall memories that never will slip.
With laughter and joy, we bask in the glow,
While the autumn leaves dance, putting on quite the show!

Where the Wild Things Fall

In the autumn breeze, leaves take flight,
Squirrels wear scarves, oh what a sight!
A raccoon in shades, striking a pose,
While acorns are tossed like tiny foes.

The winds start to giggle, they twist and twirl,
As chipmunks oink and the trees unfurl.
With laughter they dance, a whimsical spree,
Nature's odd party, come join the glee!

When pumpkins start rolling, our laughter goes wild,
And the sun in the sky looks like a child.
No worries for frost, just jokes to be told,
As we gather our cocoa, brave, hot, and bold.

So here's to the fall, where nonsense runs free,
With leaves that act silly, just wait and see!
We'll sing with the shadows, and skip in delight,
In this frolicsome dance, every day's a delight!

Changing Seasons' Embrace

Summer throws tantrums, the heat's off the charts,
While winter's slow waltz steals our snowball hearts.
Autumn comes laughing with apples galore,
And spring plays the tricks of a blooming encore.

Oh, the seasons with quirks, dressed up in their tones,
Spring brings the sunshine, but still steals our phones.
Winter sends postcards from chilly retreats,
While summer just grins, stuck in sandy seats.

The trees are confused, they giggle and sway,
"Is it time for a sweater or a beach holiday?"
Squirrels hold meetings, plan acorn affairs,
While geese waddle in, with their gossiping stares.

So let's toast the chaos, the seasons in play,
For life's a wild tour, come seize the day!
With laughter we navigate through sun and through snow,

In this fickle embrace, we find joy in the flow!

Treetop Reveries

Up in the treetops, the chatter is loud,
As the birds are all gossiping, feeling quite proud.
A llama on stilts, a raccoon in a hat,
Join squirrels in jest as they chatter and spat.

There's a squirrel who dreams of a rock and a roll,
While a wise old owl, he plays heart and soul.
The leaves whisper jokes about acorns they chase,
While the branches all nod with a melodious grace.

If trees could tell tales, oh what would we hear?
Of mischief and fun that would bring us good cheer.
With laughter so bright that it lights up the night,
In treetop reveries, everything feels right!

So come, join the fun, in the branches above,
Where nature's a party, and laughter is love!
With critters so quirky, who steal every scene,
In the treetops we laugh, and live like a dream!

The Colors of Goodbye

When trees wave goodbye in hues bright and bold,
They shout, "Don't be sad, we're just getting old!"
With a wink and a spin, the leaves twirl away,
In a burst of bright colors, they dance and they play.

Red, gold, and orange, they toss up a cheer,
As they scatter like confetti, the end of the year.
"Be happy!" they giggle, "We'll see you next fall,
With more leafy antics to share with you all!"

The skies may turn gray, but our hearts stay aglow,
With memories of colors from summer's sweet show.
As the wind starts to whistle a jazz tune of fun,
We smile at the beauty; our goodbyes have begun!

So let's celebrate change with a chuckle and shout,
For every goodbye, there's a hello about!
In the colors of autumn, we laugh and we thrive,
Embracing the humor, as long as we're alive!

The Autumnal Serenade

Leaves twirl like dancers in the breeze,
Squirrels plotting their nut-filled heists with ease.
Pumpkins whisper secrets to the chill,
While acorns fall like confetti, what a thrill!

Chilly nights bring sweaters out to play,
Hot cocoa spills in a chocolatey display.
Critters scurry, gearing for the snow,
While I just wonder where the last sip did go!

Chirp of crickets, a last serenade,
Nature's laughter, in the shades they wade.
A leaf's final pirouette on its way,
Makes me chuckle, what a funny ballet!

So here we sit, on this autumn night,
With leaves and laughter, a whimsical sight.
Let's toast to the quirks that nature brings,
As we laugh with the leaves, oh, how it sings!

Golden Hour Reflections

Sunlight casts shadows, dancing in cheer,
Squinting at life, it's funny, I fear.
Coffee spills on my favorite old jeans,
Like autumn itself, bursting at the seams!

Wind whispers gossip through trees overhead,
While I trip on twigs, just hoping I said,
Goodbye to the summer, it's time to be bold,
In sweaters and stories, new memories to mold!

Golden leaves trickle down, a confetti rain,
I laugh at a crow who's lost in his fame.
He struts like a king with a crumb in his beak,
Oh, the glory of nature, so amusingly unique!

As shadows grow long, we gather in packs,
Sharing hot apple cider, and jokingly relax.
With every laugh, another leaf takes flight,
In this funny season, life feels just right!

Symphony of Change

Rustling leaves play a tune so sweet,
While squirrels perform acrobatics, no small feat.
Nature's orchestra, with wind as the guide,
Bows twirling in colors, what a joyful ride!

The air is crisp, like a newly popped snack,
With each step I take, I hear nature's clack.
A dog barks in rhythm, chasing his tail,
As I stumble on leaves, and humor prevails!

Hats fly off like balloons escaping flight,
As gusts of wind give everyone a fright.
Laughter erupts with each clumsy plop,
In this symphony, we never want to stop!

Harvest time's here, with pies and more cheer,
Sharing smiles and stories, it's that time of year.
As the symphony plays, let our spirits rise,
Amongst the rustling leaves, we find our surprise!

The Dance of Falling Leaves

Leaves take a bow, in their winding descent,
Swirling like whirlwinds, they're heaven-sent.
Like dancers in tutus, they flutter and sway,
As I trip on a branch, what a blundering display!

The trees hold a plot, or perhaps a prank,
Each step is a gamble, like a goofy flank.
The ground is a stage for this colorful art,
Where falling leaves giggle, straight from the heart!

I twirl with delight, doing my foolish best,
With a leaf in my hair, a quirky little jest.
Nature's grand ballet is quite a delight,
In this comedy show, everything feels light!

So let's dance in the leaves, without any fear,
Embracing the chuckles that autumn brings near.
With every gust of wind, we laugh and cheer,
At the dance of the leaves, let's hold it dear!

Wind's Gentle Caress

The breeze tickles trees, dancing with flair,
Leaves giggle softly, floating on air.
Squirrels plot mischief, plotting with glee,
Chasing their tails, oh what a sight to see!

Branches sway wildly, like a funny old man,
Trying to waltz with an invisible fan.
The sun's rays chuckle, through each little crack,
Illuminating nonsense, it's hard to keep track!

Rabbits convene for a council of fun,
Arguing over who's faster to run.
The wind bursts in laughter, can't help but join,
In this leafy circus, their antics annoy!

With each gust that passes, the whole forest shakes,
Jokes in the rustle, as the laughter awakes.
Nature's a jokester, with puns like a pro,
In the wild, all creatures let their humor flow!

Echoes of the Forest Floor

Crackling twigs echo, as feet hit the ground,
The forest is chuckling, a whimsical sound.
Acorns are landing with plops here and there,
Saying 'oops, what a bumpy ride through the air!'

Frogs croak their jokes, in the soft evening light,
While fireflies misfire, a most comical sight.
Twisting and turning, they dance with delight,
In this living theater, where shadows take flight!

Mice trade their secrets in whispers of fun,
"And did you hear, the oak tree's on the run?"
They giggle and wiggle, through meadows they race,
In the shadows of giants, they find their own space!

Before the night falls and the jokes start to fade,
The whispers of laughter across all are laid.
In the echoes of critters, secrets ensue,
For humor in nature is vibrant and true!

Threading Through Gold

Wandering through foliage, dressed in bright hues,
Nature's own quilt, with layers of views.
The golden leaves chuckle, as I trip and fall,
Like an old pair of slippers, they giggle at all!

Each step a new tale, with crunches and snaps,
Squirrels give orders, like little wise chaps.
"Move to the left!" one shouts with a grin,
As I tumble and fumble—oh where to begin?

The sunbeams are plotting, a trickster's delight,
Peeking through branches, they tickle with light.
A race with shadows, I dash in pure glee,
Yet they know my next move—oh, they're laughing at me!

In this thread of gold, where silly meets wise,
Nature's humor glimmers, a feast for the eyes.
So I'll dance through the leaves, not a worry in sight,
For laughter is stitched in this autumnal delight!

The Language of Leaves

Whispering secrets in swirls and in sways,
Each leaf a comedian, in colorful plays.
They tickle the breezes with stories so bold,
Of mishaps and laughter, oh, if they could be told!

The rustle of leaves is like giggly chatter,
As branches conspire, debunking the flatter.
"Who's wearing bright colors? That's quite the affair!"
They poke fun at each other, with flair and with care!

Bushes burst into laughter, a riot of green,
As bugs join the chorus—what a sight to be seen!
Nature's own comedy, each day a new show,
Where everyone joins in, and there's plenty to know!

So next time you wander through forests so wide,
Listen closely to whispers where humor can hide.
For in the soft rustle of every tree's breath,
There's a chuckle of life, dancing on after death!

Cider and Cinnamon Dreams

In autumn's embrace, the apples are bold,
They whisper sweet secrets, their tales to be told.
With cinnamon swirls and laughter they blend,
A sip of delight, where all troubles end.

The farmers all dance, with their bushels in tow,
Claiming the fruit that they've watched grow.
But one funny fellow, with a grin ear to ear,
Came back with a pumpkin, insisting it's beer!

The cider's so fizzy, it pops like a cheer,
As friends all unite, with laughter sincere.
They toast to the mishaps, the spills and the slips,
As apples do cartwheels from overfilled hips.

So raise up your cups, let's savor the fun,
With cinnamon dreams in the warm autumn sun.
Together we'll giggle, remember the day,
Where cider and laughter just carried away!

Harvesting Light

In fields of bright colors, the harvest is here,
But finding that carrot? It fills me with fear.
I search high and low, with a furrowed brow,
When one little rabbit says, "You're lost, take a bow!"

The squash get a chuckle; they know all the tricks,
As I tumble and bumble amidst all my sticks.
Peppers are snickering, green, red, and bright,
Saying, "You might find your way, but not tonight!"

Light-hearted banter echoes through the rows,
Even the pumpkins take turns telling jokes.
As the sun starts to set, and shadows all play,
I join in their laughter, just hoping to stay.

With baskets all filled and a heart full of cheer,
We harvest a moment, a memory dear.
In fields of confusion, where friendships ignite,
Is a funny true story of harvesting light.

Serenade of Shades

The leaves all complain as the winds come to play,
Swirling like dancers who've lost their ballet.
Each color's a character, bold in their quest,
To serenade autumn, they're trying their best.

But Bert the brown leaf has lost all his sass,
He flutters and flumps, while they spin in their class.
"I'm not quite ready for this grand ballet,
Can someone please teach me? I'll have it my way!"

The reds chime in chorus, with a fiery cheer,
While yellows and oranges just twirl without fear.
Together they laugh, letting Bert know,
That shades of confusion make dancing a show!

As twilight approaches, the stage starts to fade,
The merry leaf dancers now laugh and then raid,
With every last gust, they twinkle their shade,
In a serenade softly, the colors they played.

Echoes of the Past

In the woods there's a tale whispered soft in the breeze,
Of squirrels stealing acorns with absolute ease.
As autumn replays all the follies of yore,
These echoes remind us of such mischief and more.

Old owl up high has a penchant for jokes,
While acorns are giggling, it's quite a hoax.
The memories tumble like leaves off the trees,
Each rustle a chuckle in the warm autumn freeze.

Yet down by the stream, the frogs croak their rhymes,
Recalling past pranks from the good olden times.
"Hey, remember the bee that stole all our jam?
We covered it up with a giant green ham!"

With echoes of laughter, and eyes wide with dreams,
We gather the stories that twist like the beams.
In shadows of whimsy, we dance with the past,
In a world full of echoes that forever will last.

www.ingramcontent.com/pod-product-compliance
Lightning Source LLC
Chambersburg PA
CBHW071818160426
43209CB00003B/128